Timmy Marches On

Timmy Marches On

Rose Stilwell
Illustrator Hannah Sierra

Book 2 - How Timmy Grew Series

Copyright

Timmy Marches On
Book 2 of 3 - How Timmy Grew Series

This educational book offers guidance as children grow and begin school based on a fictional account. The events and characters herein are imaginary, do not refer to specific places or persons.
The opinions expressed in this manuscript are solely the opinions of the author and do not represent those of the publisher. The author has represented and warranted ownership and/or legal right to publish all the materials in this book.
Timmy Marches On
All Rights Reserved.
Copyright © 2022 Rose Stilwell V-1.0
This book may not be reproduced, transmitted, or stored in whole or in part by any means, including graphic, electronic, or mechanical without the express written consent of the publisher except brief quotations embodied in critical articles and reviews.
Nova Publishing, Bakersfield, California

Dedication

I would like to dedicate this book to all of my family members, complete with my great, great grandchildren!

I am also dedicating it to all my faithful friends and followers.

God bless you everyone.

Table of Contents

1	I'm Back	Page 1
2	Surprise and Shock	Page 3
3	Books…Books…Books	Page 6
4	Laughter and Tears	Page 10
5	Summertime	Page 13
6	Moving Right Along	Page 18
7	Reading and Thinking	Page 23
8	Please Not This?	Page 26
9	Another Summer	Page 29
10	Surprise	Page 34
11	Great or Not So Great	Page 36
12	Don't Worry Be Happy	Page 41
13	The Dreaded Returns	Page 43
14	More Times More	Page 45

15	A Lot Of Stuff	Page 46
16	Art At Last	Page 48
17	Happiness and Sorrow	Page 52
18	Another Summer	Page 58
19	Frustration Steps In	Page 62
20	Fourth Grade Begins	Page 64
21	Kind Of Rules	Page 66
22	A Smile and A K!	Page 68
23	Learning Our Country	Page 69
24	Reading and Writing	Page 71
25	Everything Else	Page 73
26	Where Will We Go	Page 75
27	Wait and See	Page 80
28	A Fantastic Shock	Page 81
29	Love and Joy	Page 82

30	Please Not Now!	Page 84
31	Recess Talk and Play	Page 86
32	Kindness	Page 87
33	Happiness Shared	Page 89
34	School Continues	Page 91
35	Discussion Time	Page 92
36	Another Summer	Page 95
37	Wow!	Page 96
38	Unimageable Fun	Page 98
39	The Sights We Saw	Page 100
40	A New Day	Page 104
41	Help Please	Page 108
42	Struggle and Learn	Page 112
43	Awards, Tears and A Step Up	Page 115
44	A Long Look Back	Page 116

45 Another Summer	Page 117
Epilogue	Page 119
My Thank You	Page 122

Preface

Welcome Back to Timmy's World!

I am returning with a prayer and a promise to continue. Please take a trip with Timmy (I mean Super Smart Timmy) as he continues to grow in size and knowledge.

As your child continues through school, the parents help is sometimes essential. There is always homework to complete, with perhaps a little push from parents. Spelling, reading and math will always be a part of the child's education.

Love, laughter and sometimes tears are a part of everyone's life. As the author I would like to share a poem I wrote a few years ago for my grown children.

THIS IS HAPPINESS!

As we walk thru life
Whether short or long

We have a great family
Which helps make us strong

As I get older, my blessings
continue to flow

Marriage and birth, family,
and joy. continue to grow

As we grow and our numbers increase
We hope these wonders will never cease

We each have memories we like to share
For a few of mine I will take you there

I love you all so very much
For the blessings of my life
I feel God's touch

    I hope you will be blessed and enjoy TIMMY MARCHES ON, as much as I have enjoyed writing it!

Chapter One

I'm Back

I'm back! I have so much to tell you!

Kindergarten was wonderful! Our teacher, who was really great, read us stories about so many things. My favorite was "WHERE THE WILD THINGS ARE" by Maurice Sendak. The whole class liked the stories about "CLIFFORD THE BIG RED DOG" by Norman Bridwell.

After we finished the first Clifford story each child drew a picture of Clifford with crayons on a white sheet of construction paper. It was a lot of fun and funny. Everyone got to show their picture to the class and tell something about Clifford. Then our teacher put them all up on the walls. Clifford would not have recognized himself. Would you believe this, my mom still has that picture! That is, with the hundreds of other pictures and items!

Learning, reading, having fun, dancing, and making friends. It was so much fun. What a great beginning of my travels through school.

Chapter Two

Surprise and Shock

Summer was soon over with memories of all the fun vacations with Jimmy and his family, and just living happily. And then came September! Jimmy and I had talked about it, and we decided we had aced kindergarten so what would be different about first grade. After all, we were SMART. Just ask our moms and dads. Were WE in for a surprise!

As we all know, time marches on and the day came for Jimmy and me to go back to school and enter first grade.

I could see the difference as soon as I walked in with my friend Jimmy. There were no tables to sit around, only desks. Each desk had a name tag on it, and we had to find our name and sit down.

If I hadn't been such a big smart boy, I would have cried. Jimmy's desk was clear across the room from mine! We always sat together in kindergarten, and this was not fair!! We knew how to behave and not talk when the teacher said to please pay attention.

That wasn't the only bad thing, there was a girl on each side of me. Who wants to sit by a girl? They were kinda cute though.

Mrs. Brill (that was her name) looked nice, a little like my grandmother because her hair was gray. She told us to place our right hand on our heart and we would say the Pledge of Allegiance.

A few of the kids did not know their right hand from their left! This was hard for me to understand. Had they forgotten what they learned in kindergarten? So, our first day began with the flag salute and roll taking.

You will not believe what Mrs. Brill did next. "First things first," she said.

Then she passed out MATH papers (she called it arithmetic). You know how I feel about math. YUCK! I guess she wanted to know how much we knew about math because the paper was filled with simple addition problems. I breathed a sigh of relief and I thought, I can do this. The math was easy, which was nice.

After collecting the papers our teacher passed out books by rows. There was a book for each child. The first book was a reading book. The teacher said that we could look at our new book while she was busy. The class was very quiet while Mrs. Brill corrected our math papers. I think everyone got a star on their paper. I know I did.

In a few minutes, after our teacher had corrected the papers, she stood with a smile. Then she praised the class for their good work and how quiet we had been. "I am so glad I have a class full of students who know how to behave in school!" Mrs. Brill said. I was thinking that I was glad to have a nice teacher like Mrs. Brill! Everyone looked happy as we continued our day.

Chapter Three

Books…Books…More Books

As my story moves on, the teacher and a helper (she chose Jimmy) passed out more books. I don't know why she didn't ask me! Maybe next time.

BOOKS, BOOKS, and more books. Besides the reading books, there were science books, math books and several others I can't remember. These were heavy books and we had to place them in our desks, very carefully. That wasn't all, there were workbooks for each subject.

Mrs. Brill told us to take out our reading books again and read the first story quietly. It was very easy to read and very short. But it wasn't a story about Dick and Jane that my mom had told me about.

Our teacher was very nice! She said, "You have worked very quietly and now let's learn something about each other." She told us she was married and had four grown children. I told you she seemed a little old. She also had grandchildren.

Then, starting a row at a time, each child stood in front of the class and told something about themselves. Some told about where they lived and how they got to school. A few walked to school if they lived close. Others rode the bus. A few were driven to school by their parents.

Many talked about their families, and a few told us about their pets. Speaking about pets. I thought that a pet was a dog or cat. I learned something new that day. One little girl said her family lived in an apartment and couldn't have a dog or cat, so her parents bought her some goldfish. She said how fun it was to see them swim to the top of the water to get the food as she dropped it in. She told us that when they moved to a house, she would keep her fish, and her parents promised her a puppy.

I really like dogs and cats; I have a dog like Lassie. I suppose fish would be fine too.

I don't know if this was a joke or the truth – but one boy said his family had a snake! He said it was not very big and he called it a corn snake. YUK!! Who would want a snake?

It finally came my turn. As I stood in front of the teacher and my classmates, I was quiet for a minute. Then I told them about my best friend Jimmy and a few of the things we had done together. I also told them that we always sat side by side in kindergarten and now I could not sit by him. No, I did not cry. I was too big!

When the bell rang for recess Mrs. Brill asked if she could talk to Jimmy and me. The first thing she said was that it was nice to have a best friend in the same classroom. "I can change the desks around if you want to sit together," she said. Then she asked us a question. "If I allow you to sit beside each other will you be able to sit quietly while I am teaching a lesson?" Our answer came quickly. Yes, we can, was our response. Our parents had already talked to us about good behavior in school and to have respect for the teacher. We told her that we were smart and would follow the rules. GOOD NEWS! When we came in from recess, she had moved our desks and we were beside one another.

We soon found out that you must earn your privileges. A few weeks later we were talking instead of listening and I was back with the girls.

Lesson well taught and lesson well learned. We apologized and were well behaved for the next two weeks. Then, what we all look for, a second chance. We were back together and VERY quiet.

Chapter Four

Laughter and Tears

Mrs. Brill was very nice and seemed happy to be our teacher. She wasn't the only happy person in the classroom.

One morning she spelled a word wrong on the board and a girl raised her hand and said, "Did you spell that word wrong?"

Let me tell you why we loved our teacher. She looked back at what she had written and started laughing! "You are right," she said, "that word is spelled wrong."

Then Mrs. Brill said, "Everyone makes mistakes." That is a statement I will always remember. I am guilty of making mistakes, what I do, what I say and many more. I remembered many mistakes I had made in math, perhaps because I did not like it, but I did try as hard as I could.

I still remember a HUGE mistake I made that was never caught. This is very hard to admit...I cheated. You know by now that I do not like math. We were having a test and I looked over at Jimmy's work and wrote down his answer on my paper.

Several weeks later I was still feeling guilty about it. I went home after school and told my parents about it. Mom said she was pleased that I trusted them enough to tell them. Dad said I would have to tell Mrs. Brill what I had done.

The next morning, I got to school a little early to tell my teacher what I had done. With tears in my eyes I said, "Mrs. Brill, I cheated on a test."

She said softly, "Thank you for telling me. It takes a strong person to admit a mistake." Then she gave me a big hug. That was forgiveness!

Mrs. Brill's mistake was an accident, mine was deliberate and that is the difference. Mistakes are part of life, and we can learn by them. I tried harder to listen and learn the things my teacher taught.

With a lot of help from my great parents my math began to get better, and I started to understand it more.

Growing taller and better looking (I had to add that line) it was soon time for my adventures in second grade.

But now it's time for our summer to begin!

Chapter Five

Summertime!!!

We are going to have so much fun. We thought we would.......but what will we do first?

"Do you want to play catch?" Jimmy asked. I said, "OK" but it really did not sound like very much fun to me. We played for a little while, but it wasn't much fun in a backyard. The school playground was so big that you could throw the ball HARD.

"Let's throw a basketball and see who can put the most balls in the hoop," I suggested. "That sounds good," was Jimmy's answer. That lasted about 30 minutes. "Now what do we do?" asked Jimmy.

We went to Jimmy's house to talk to his mom. "We're bored," we told her. "Really," she said, "This is your first day of vacation. How can you be bored?"

"There's nothing fun to do around here!" "I have something you can do," his mom said, "so you won't be bored." "What," we shouted.

"Go clean the weeds out of that flower bed for me." What could we do? It sounded like an order, so we went outside again.

We spent an HOUR outside pulling weeds! Timmy's mom came to the back door and said, "Are you still bored?" "NO!" we said. "Great," she said,

"Why don't you come inside and have some lemonade and cookies?" That sounded good to me.

After finishing the CHOCOLATE CHIP COOKIES, I said I was going home and read a book for a little while. It would be a book about Lassie. I didn't say I was tired, but I think his mom knew. She said she thought that was a good idea and Jimmy could read for a while too.

I told you that I had a dog like Lassie, but my dog was a boy, so I named him Laddie. This was a name from a book about Lassie. Let me tell you that getting a dog was not easy! I asked and asked, and this is the answer I received.

"I want a dog," I said to my dad.

He looked at me and said,
"That's really too bad!"
I asked, "Why can't I have a pet?"
Dad said, "You're not old enough yet."
"How old do you have to be?" I asked.
His answer was "Well, let me see…
Old enough to care for a life not your own,
You can't just throw a dog a bone.
You must love him and pet him
And care for his needs,
It will not always be fun,
It's a job that's never done."
I answered, "Please get me a dog and you will see, I will love him like you love me!"
And that is how I got Laddie!
I love to read my books about Lassie. I have a bunch of them…LASSIE…LASSIE COME HOME…SON OF LASSIE…LASSIE TO THE RESCUE…AND many more. I read until I fell asleep.
Three months of having fun! I hoped it would start soon. IT DID!

Things were looking up! Our parents decided it was time for us to learn how to swim. They were going to take us to a swim school. Now that sounded like fun. We hoped!

Our families had been to the beach many times, but we only waded in the surf. I wasn't sure if I wanted to swim in the ocean.

Jimmy and I were a little worried about swimming, but of course, we had to go to swim school.

Neither Jimmy nor I had ever been in a pool, and it looked big and DEEP. I asked my mom if she was going to go in the water with me. She said no but she would be right by the side of the pool.

The class started with everyone holding on to the side of the pool and kicking their feet. Every day we learned a little more and it was beginning to be fun. Until we were learning to float.

The teacher always kept her hand under my back. Until she took it away, and down I went. I guess she thought I would just stand up in the shallow water, but I didn't. After I went under twice, she pulled me up.

When I finished coughing, I began to cry. That was the end of that day's swimming. I told mom I was not going back! The teacher said she was sorry, but I was not sure I could trust her anymore.

Well, I went back. I guess the best thing that happened was that I was not afraid of water anymore. AND I learned to swim. This lesson would last forever.

Our summer was great! Trips together with our families. Universal Studios, Disneyland again and many other places. Two boys could not have had a better summer.

Before summer was over, we were both ready to go back to school. We wanted to see our friends and learn new things.

Chapter Six

Moving Right Along

Because life never stands still, mine moved on.

Here we go again. Second grade and Jimmy and I were in the same room. Several of our friends from first grade were also there.

On the door was a sign saying ROOM 6. I laughed to myself as I remembered the time I came home from Jimmy's house and there was a sign on my bedroom door.

I hope you remember it too. It was the beginning of my reading skills. Words to sentences......to books.......to school and now to second grade. Does life always go this fast?

New teacher, new rules, new students, and new books. A new school year was beginning.

First, let me tell you about our teacher.

She looked very young, and she told us that it was her first year to teach school. She looked as frightened as we felt. This was our first year in second grade! Jimmy raised his hand and told her we would help her! That brought a big smile to her face, and everyone smiled with her. We were off to a good start.

Her name was Miss Love. What a nice name. It really suited her because she showed her love for her students and teaching many times.

After roll call and the flag salute we got down to business. She asked the class what we should do first. Someone said that classes always have rules. She wrote the kids suggestions on the board as they offered them. We said that we should behave, be nice, listen and always raise our hands before speaking out. There were probably 10 or more.

"Let's make this simpler because I am going to have to make a chart about them so we will remember," she said.

She may have been new, but she was smart! She said, "Let's use the word think." Then she explained what she meant. This is what she told us. I will let you read it yourself because I have thought about it many times.

THINK

T   Is it true?
H   Is it helpful?
I   Is it inspiring?
N   Is it necessary?
K   Is it kind?

We all agreed that this was good, and we should always remember it, especially the K, is it kind. The next morning, she had written it on a chart and placed it in the front of the room. This was a great start to our second-grade year, and one we would carry away in our hearts.

My desk and Jimmy's were not together but we never said a word about it. Then about four weeks later we came to school and all the desks had been moved. Jimmy and I were side by side again. Didn't I tell you Miss Love was smart. She had noticed the friends that were together on the playground at recess and many desks of friends had been placed together. She remembered what the K stood for.

We better get back to school! We need to get back to the first day. There were books to pass out and put away. More subjects, more workbooks and then our own binder to keep our work in. Miss Love said we should keep our desk clean all the time. No clutter. I did not think that would be hard because I had to keep my whole room clean at home. Then the bell rang, and it was recess time.

Jimmy and I ran around the track one time and then we sat down on the grass. It was a long way around it. Several of our first-grade friends came over and sat with us. What do you think of our new teacher someone asked? Someone else said she was going to need help because she had not taught before. One boy said we could really help her because this was our third year at school (counting kindergarten). We really needed to use the K because that would help.

No one thought about the many years Miss Love had been in school! Think about it, we were only in the second grade. She had many more memories about her days in school than we did.

The good thing was that we were all willing to help.

Chapter Seven

Reading and Thinking

When we came in from recess, our teacher asked us to please take out our reading books and turn to the first story. Each child would read one paragraph. It went from one student to the next and if they missed a word, she would softly tell them the word. Once again, she was teaching us about the K.

The story was short, and the class listened to it several times until everyone had read. Miss Love said, "Please put your books away." Then she asked,

"What was the story about?" Several hands went up and she called on Mary.

Of course, Mary knew what the story was about and answered the teacher's question. The next thing the teacher asked was, "What happened in the beginning?"

Again, several hands went up and the teacher called on Sam. He told the class something that was in the story. Miss Love said, "That was very good, but what happened before that in the story?"

Fewer hands went up and then she called on me. I told her what happened before that and she said, "Yes, that happened in the story also, but what happened first in the story, in the beginning, on the first page?"

Finally, the class understood what she was asking. Again, up came more hands. The question was answered correctly.

What happened in the middle of the story was the next question. Well, lots of things happened in the middle of the story. There were probably at least five answers to that one.

There were only a few more questions for the class to answer. What happened at the end of the story? Was it a happy story or a sad one? Did you like it? Would you like to write a happy story?

We all said yes, but we didn't know she meant NOW!

She passed out lined paper to the class and told us to write one paragraph of something happy we remembered. "This is how stories are sometimes started, the author has a memory to share," she said.

Miss Love continued, "If I was writing a paragraph, I would write about going to see the ocean for the first time. It was so much fun watching the waves come in, some large and some small." "Please do your best," the teacher told us.

My memory was clear about many happy times, but it was hard to write them down. I do know that writing will be fun when I learn a little more. Like how to spell words!

When we were finished it was time for lunch and then playing until the bell rang.

Chapter Eight

Please Not This!

MATH TIME! We opened our math books and the first few pages looked easy. They were a repeat of our first-grade work.

Finally, it happened. I realized that adding and subtracting went together. They were just the opposite of each other. Like 9+8 = 17 and 17–8 = 9. The same three numbers used a different way. How easy is that.

Wow! What an eye opener. I had finally caught on. I told my mom and dad about it when I got home. They were so happy that I was beginning to understand math.

My reading skills were beginning to pay off. We were starting to do word problems. I won't say I hated them because that is not really nice, but (new word) I despised them. Being able to read well helped me to understand the problem but I still had to get the right answer. I remembered something my dad had told me, NEVER GIVE UP, so I tried and sometimes I was successful.

Then Miss Love did something I will always love her for. She put two students together, one a good reader and one who was good in math.

I would read the problem out loud, and we would talk about what we needed to do to solve it. Then my partner would show me how to do the math. Miss Love was one smart teacher! We not only worked well together, but we became friends.

Recess was a happy time for me. It wasn't always happy for a few of the students. If their homework wasn't turned in and finished, they would have to sit outside the door and work on it while others played.

Some shed a few tears, finished their work, and went to play. Some were just mad and refused to work on the papers. Guess what! They spent the next recess in the same place with the same paper. They also got a note home to parents which had to be signed and returned the next day.

You think our teacher was mean? NO, she was teaching them that life has many rules to follow. Not following rules always has consequences. Theirs was only a few minutes of play lost. When you are grown and refuse to follow the rules the consequences are much greater.

Our teacher that year was special. She praised when it was deserved and scolded softly when that was needed.

One thing she always did was give us her time. Always available to answer questions and give individual help when needed. As a class I believe we tried to rise to her standards because we felt her love for us.

Even the angry kids began to smile and enjoy the class. They even brought their homework in on time. No more students outside the door, only happy faces on the playground.

An unforgettable teacher and an unforgettable year.

Chapter Nine

Another Summer

This summer started out a little differently than the last one. Dad said we were going to Missouri to see his aunt who was getting very old. We had been there when I was very small, and I did not remember it. I asked dad if we were going to take Laddie along. He told me that the trip was too long, and Jimmy and his mom and dad would take care of him. I gave him a big hug before I got in the car. I sure hated to leave him.

Mom and dad took turns driving on Route 66. There were so many new things to see. Deserts and mountains, cacti, and trees, all were beautiful in their own way.

Mom asked if I remembered the story about Bambi the deer. She said to keep watch as we might see some deer by the road. Sure enough, she was right, only a few minutes later we saw a doe and her fawn standing by the roadside. What an amazing scene. If you have never seen an animal in the wild, you have missed a beautiful sight.

There was so much to see! I was glad we were in the car when we saw a snake crossing the road. Dad pulled over and we watched out the closed windows as it completed its journey. IT WAS A RATTLE SNAKE!

We stopped for lunch in a small town. I don't remember the name, but we sure ate well. We had Hot Pork Sandwiches. This was a first for me, but they were good. Filled to the brim, we traveled for several hours, and I fell asleep. Mom woke me up and told me we were going to stop and have some watermelon. There was a little stand ahead and dad asked if I would like to try a watermelon with a yellow center? I laughed. "Dad, you know watermelons are red inside," I said. "Wait and see," he said. Dad was right and the inside was yellow, and it was delicious.

Dad told us a lot about his aunt and the happy trips his family had taken when he was small. Aunt Mary was always waiting with a smile and a hug for everyone. I had looked at a picture of her but didn't remember her.

He described the leaning fence and the huge tree in her front yard which had mistletoe hanging from it. The smell of lilacs was everywhere. I could hardly wait to see this place until he told us she had no inside toilet and no running water.

She got her water from a well with a large pump. Dad said it was the best water he had ever tasted and ice cold even in the hot summer. It came from an underground spring. He told us about her garden and orchard and her blackcap raspberry bushes which were very thorny. That did not stop her from picking them and she made pies and jelly from the berries. I could almost see it in my mind as he talked about it. He told us she was a great cook too.

On the third day we reached the small town where dad's aunt lived. Dad honked the horn as we arrived, and she ran out the door to greet us. Oh, the hugs, kisses, and tears that followed. I found out she WAS a great cook the next morning. We had bacon, eggs, homemade biscuits, and blackcap raspberry jelly. Let me tell you, if you have never tasted blackcap raspberry jelly you have really missed a treat!

This was an amazing town! Everyone knew everyone else, and they were so friendly. When we went to the little store in town to buy groceries you would have thought celebrities had come. "Is this your family from California?" the storekeeper asked our aunt. They all knew we were coming!

Have you ever been to a small town in the Midwest? I don't know if it is the same, but this one was wonderful! Most of the people walked everywhere. They learned our names quickly and always greeted us with a smile. They all seemed to have gardens unless they were unable to. These people never went without vegetables. Friends kept them well supplied. They talked together, laughed together, cried in sorrow together, and played together. Horseshoes and croquet were played in the daylight and sometimes cards at night.

We stayed a week and then began our trip home. The rest of the summer was spent doing many things and going places with Jimmy's family.

Chapter 10

Surprise!

It was the first day of third grade. The students were lined up at the door. We were anxious to watch the door open and see Mrs. Smith who was to be our new teacher.

Well, that was a surprise! Instead of young Mrs. Smith, who we all thought we were going to have, an elderly lady, (I don't want to say old), opened the door. She looked more like someone's grandma than a teacher. She smiled and opened the door wide and told us to please come in.

We sat down quietly, as we were not sure what was happening. I thought maybe she was the aide and Mrs. Smith would be coming in shortly.

She told us her name was Mrs. Scott and she would be our teacher. She explained that Mrs. Smith had become ill and had to undergo surgery. She would not be back until after Christmas vacation.

Ouch, I thought. Everyone knew Mrs. Smith was nice but we had never seen or heard about Mrs. Scott before. Would she be nice or grouchy? Mean or sweet? Only time would tell.

Chapter 11

Great or Not So Great?

I looked at Jimmy and he looked back with raised eyebrows and shrugged his shoulders.

Like the beginning of every school day, the class stood and recited the Pledge of Allegiance. Next, Mrs. Scott took roll and with a smile she said we looked like a great class.

She said that she had talked to Mrs. Smith, and she had said she was very sorry she could not be our teacher for a while but would be back after Christmas. I thought to myself, that is a long time.

Mrs. Scott asked if we would like to write her a get well note? Raise your hands if you would like to do that. We all raised our hands and she said, "Good, I purchased some nice note cards for you to use."

Her next instructions were that to make sure that the cards were nicely done we should write what we wanted to say on some unlined paper she would pass out.

Then we could be sure that the spelling was correct, and our handwriting was well done. We needed to practice because we were not used to writing on unlined paper and the note cards had no lines.

We only needed to write two or three sentences, Mrs. Scott told us, as the cards were small. She hesitated a second and then said she thought two sentences would be fine as we had to have room to sign our names. She said that this would be a sample.

"Will you check them for us?" asked Jimmy. Mrs. Scott told us of course she would do that while we were at recess. We were ready to start, almost.

Then Judy raised her hand and asked the question we all wanted to ask. "What will I say? I have never done this before." Our teacher said she had not thought about that. She said, "Let's put some ideas on the board." Several hands were raised.

One student said he was sorry she was sick. Another said get well soon and then someone said we would miss her. One girl said we would work hard for her until she came back.

"These are all good ideas," the teacher said. "Please write what you want to say and remember, two sentences only and sign your name."

It took a while for everyone to finish and then it was recess time. There wasn't too much playing because we were talking about Mrs. Scott. Was third grade going to be fun and would she be nice. We all thought she was nice, but we wondered if she would be too strict. "We'll soon see," said Jimmy.

As we entered our classroom and sat down Mrs. Scott asked us a question. "How many of you did your very best on your note?" Only two hands were raised, and neither one was mine. "Thank you for being honest," she said.

"Let me tell you a story," she told us. "Once upon a time, when I was in first grade, I had a pretty strict but loving teacher. As she walked around the room looking at what the children were writing she would sometimes stop and say, Is that your best work? If the answer was no, she would ask what should you do?" The answer was always the same, Do It Over! "Thank you," was her response.

"Please listen carefully to what I am about to say. I am here to give you my best and I expect you to do the same for me. This will make us both happy and doing your best will help you as you continue your education."

"I will not have you start over because I have corrected your writing and will have you use it to write your note again. We will have thirty minutes to complete them and the two who have no mistakes will have free reading time." Then she said, "How many will do their best? Remember, this is not for me, but for you, to help you make a success of your life." Every hand was raised.

As I think back, I will always remember her words. This is not for me but for you, to help you make a success of your life. What a great statement!

Thirty minutes was up, and we turned in our papers. "Thank you," the teacher said. "I will read them while you read the first chapter in your Social Studies book. We will discuss this reading later after I look over your BEST work."

About twenty minutes later she was finished and stood before the class with a smile. "Well done," she stated, "You are ready to complete your notecards." You would not believe how quiet the class was as they worked on their cards. By the time they were finished it was time for lunch. A few would say what a waste of time. All morning spent over cards! I say HOORAY FOR A TEACHER LIKE MRS. SCOTT! A lesson learned that will not be forgotten.

After lunch was over, we did not have to spend time wondering if our teacher was nice and not a bit grouchy. We knew she was! We spent the rest of lunchtime smiling and playing. We played volleyball, kick ball and tether ball. We shared our time, our smiles, and our friendship.

Chapter 12

Don't Worry, Be Happy

A lot of hot and happy kids lined up to go into class. Mrs. Scott asked us to sit down and cool off. While we were quiet, she told us we had something important to discuss.

"Did everyone notice how nice the room was decorated?" she said. "I did not do this," she told us. "Mrs. Smith had it ready before she became ill. It looks great, doesn't it?" We all agreed that it did.

"There is one thing that bothers me though. The list of rules on the front board. That looks like a lot! Let's erase them and start over." The class liked that because we had looked at them too and there were a lot.

"Will someone please help me decide what rules we really need," she said. The hands flew up. Be good… Don't hit anyone…Do your work, and on and on. When Mrs. Scott had written them on the board, we had fifteen! More than before.

"That looks terrible," she said.

"I can't remember all of these, and we need the board to write on." Let me think a minute. The class was quiet while she had her head down and was thinking. "I got it!"

What does she mean, I thought? "I think I know one rule that will cover all these," she said. How could that be I thought. She wrote these words on the board. TREAT OTHERS LIKE YOU WANT TO BE TREATED! Then she went down the list and asked us if it covered each one and it did.

Did everyone always follow this rule? Of course not! That is not real life. However, we had three chances. Our first offence, our name was put on the board. The second time there was a check by our name. We were careful because the third time there was a note home to parents which had to be signed and returned. If the note was not brought back, there was a phone call to parents. No one wanted a note or call home.

Chapter 13

The Dreaded Returns

Math time again! I was still struggling and even with the help I got at home it was not clicking.

And then I heard some more news. We were going to learn our multiplication tables. ADD…SUBTRACT…NOW SOMETHING NEW! Well, I thought, I can never do this! Never is a long time.

Mrs. Scott said, "Everybody in third grade must learn this." This was one time I really did want to shed a few tears. But I did not want anyone to call me a baby! So, I made myself listen.

"How much is 2+2?" she said. I perked up, that is easy, I thought. Next, what is 2x2? A boy raised his hand and asked what did she mean? She explained it was the same answer but a new way to use numbers and this x between the numbers was called multiplication. Let's try 2x3. It is asking the same as 3+3. The answer to both was 6 of course. This did not seem so hard, just another way of writing it. She had written some on the board and then asked what looked different about them. That is right was her statement as someone said it was the sign in the middle. The X is the multiplication sign, and you will get used to seeing it.

I have a chart with the multiplication table of 2 for you to look at and think about she told us. It was very large, and she placed it on the front board so we could see and study it.

After a few minutes she told us that we already knew the first two tables. A hand was raised, and the question was asked, you only showed us one! Mrs. Scott laughed. "Why would I show you the ones times table when you already know that? What is 1x1?" she said. The class laughed and every hand was raised. It even seemed a little easier to me and I was not so scared of something new.

Chapter 14

More Times More

Everyone has struggles in this life and I was having a lot of them! It seemed there was more multiplied by more. Besides multiplication, we had two-digit addition and two-digit subtraction. I continued to struggle with math. Learning the multiplication tables was hard but I had always been good at memorizing. I was soon able to do that. Being able to use them was another story.

To make matters worse, Mrs. Scott started giving us word problems. I am not blaming her for the math, it was all from the math and workbooks. Let's talk about this later as I am SICK of math!

Did I say more? You got it. Our next subject was Language Arts.

Chapter 15

A Lot of Stuff

Language Arts! It didn't look like art to me. Why don't they just say reading, writing, speaking and whatever.

Let me say this. I LOVE to read! I don't mind writing, but I need a lot of practice. Writing a book report was kind of fun because I was telling about a good book I had read, and what it was about. Mrs. Scott was very nice, but couldn't that have been enough? I guess not for her. She told the class the next book report would be an oral one.

If you have ever been there, you will know what I mean. This was so hard! As I look back, I wonder why. I was in front of friends, and I knew the story. I did the best I could and was about to sit down when the teacher asked if there were any questions. Several hands went up and I heard the same questions that I had heard before from the teacher.

What happened first? What happened next? What happened last? What were the names of the people in the story? What part did I like best? I saw a few smirks on some faces when they asked these questions. What they didn't think about was that they also had to make an oral book report very soon. Was I ready for them? You bet I was. This may be wrong, but it was payback time!

Next on Mrs. Scott's list was proper punctuation. That is not hard. You start a sentence with a capital letter and end with a punctuation mark. Knowing where to put the commas was not so easy.

We discussed parts of speech. We all knew what a noun and a verb were. We begin to hear about pronouns, adverbs, and adjectives. Is there never an end? I have never found it. I asked my mom that question a long time ago and I remembered she said no, there was always something new to learn.

Chapter 16

Art at Last

This was a special time. Colored pencil sets were passed to all the students. I got to help! We learned something new about Mrs. Scott. She was very talented in drawing, and we could tell she loved it.

Before we began the lesson we went outside and looked around. There was a giant tree and she talked about it, "Does this tree start flat on the ground? No, look where the trunk has several sections where it goes into the ground. This is the roots that go WAY down to hold the tree up."

There were several large branches that we could see. "Can you count how many small branches come from the big ones?" she asked us. No was our answer. "Are any of the branches the same? Does this tree look like the tree beside it?"

Mrs. Scott said, "Of course not, trees are a little like people, none are exactly alike." We looked around one more time and went back to our room.

We were ready to begin. We were to watch her first and then draw one part at a time. She started drawing a tree. She began with the trunk and then added some branches. "Please draw a tree trunk on your paper. Then draw some branches. Remember to leave space at the top of the paper for the rest of the tree."

She told us that she was only going to put a few smaller branches on her tree, but we could put as many as we wanted. Our teacher walked around the room and admired our work. Walking back to the board she told us that her tree looked bare. "Have you ever seen a tree like that?" Most of the kids said, 'yes in the winter'.

"Good answers," she said and smiled, "Let's make our trees summer trees with lots of leaves."

Finished? Not quite. The trunk and branches were all one color in her picture, and she said something was wrong.

Back outside we went. "Look at the trunk, is it all the same color?" she asked.

We noticed it was darker on one side and she told us that side was in the shade.

There were also other colors we could see and think about. We went back and finished our trees and put our names on the back. The teacher said we would finish our pictures tomorrow as it was time to go home. We thought they were finished!

The next morning, after The Pledge of Allegiance, and roll we were in for a surprise.

"Let's take a break and finish our pictures." What a teacher! First, she showed us some pictures that others had painted, and we looked at them carefully. Our pictures didn't have any ground around the trees. There was some grass here and there and even flowers in the pictures she showed us. That looked good.

Mrs. Scott said, "Your trees look great and now you can finish them and put your name on the bottom front like real artists do." She would give us twenty minutes and then she would pick them up. "DON'T FORGET YOUR NAMES."

Then she smiled and said, "Be Happy. because next comes math!" She had to do her job right too.

The weeks seemed to pass by quickly, too quickly! Mrs. Scott never gave up on us. She put us in groups of 4 so we could discuss a play that we were going to do in class. A few had a part in the play and others would be the audience. Everyone had a copy of the play and helped the actors to memorize their parts.

What a show of teamwork. With no props, and no costumes, the play went on. No one missed a line. These were not just spoken lines, but a true telling of the story. You would have had to be there to see what happened next.

The clapping was tremendous, and then it happened. One student stood up and continued to clap. It became a standing ovation as everyone stood and clapped. It was better than a Broadway production! Love, love, love seemed to be the motto of our class.

Chapter 17

Happiness and Sorrow

It seemed to happen so quickly that we were not ready for it. December was here. We all knew what was going to happen. Mrs. Scott would not be back after Christmas.

Was this part of the growing up process? We were going to lose someone that we loved.

We all knew who Mrs. Smith was and had heard she was a nice teacher. But she wasn't Mrs. Scott. No one could take her place.

School continued as usual, but this was always on our minds. We talked about what we could do for her at recess, how could we let her know how we felt?

A small part of our question was solved one afternoon. Mrs. Scott had to take a break to use the restroom. The vice principal took her place while she was gone. She said, "We have to do this quickly before your teacher comes back." She passed out a sheet of lined paper to each one and said, "Put it in your desk. Take it home and write a letter to Mrs. Scott thanking her for being your teacher. When you have finished, please bring them to my office and I will put them together with a cover sheet so she can keep them forever."

It seemed that the whole school was going to miss her. She always had a smile and a kind word for everyone.

The last two weeks were difficult for the class, and I am sure for Mrs. Scott. The kids were bringing her presents and she opened them and said thank you. On Wednesday a boy walked to her desk and said quietly, "I don't have a present for you." She stood up, smiled, and said, "Of course you do." The boy looked astonished and said, "What?" Opening her arms she said, "You brought me a big hug!"

I wish you could see how his face lit up as he hugged her back. I don't believe a smile left his face the whole day. There's always a way to show love and to receive it.

Jimmy and I had been talking about what we could get Mrs. Scott for Christmas for a long time. We both had been saving our allowance for weeks but didn't know what to buy her. We decided to talk to our moms about it.

Well, Jimmy's mom said, "We know we see her at church every Sunday. How about a necklace with a cross on it?"

Both of us liked that and the last week of school before Christmas vacation we went shopping. THEY TOOK US TO A JEWELRY STORE. We looked and looked, and everything was too expensive. A very nice clerk came to help us, and we told her what we were looking for. "I think I can help you," she said. She found a small cross on a tiny chain. It was still too much but our mom's chipped in and we bought the cross.

The clerk placed it in a lovely box and then wrapped it with gold color paper and put a big red bow on it! Wow! Were we happy! Then she gave us a card and envelope to go with our gift. Jimmy wrote Mrs. Scott on the envelope (his writing was a little better than mine) and we both signed the card.

On Monday we were ready to go. When we got to her room several students were already there and her desk was filled with gifts. Before she opened the gifts, she told us that we had already given her the very best gift. The love she had felt in the classroom could never be lost or stolen and would last forever! I don't think there was a dry eye in the class, including Mrs. Scott.

Every gift was a good gift. Whether it was a flower picked on the way to school or our cross, her response was the same, thank you and I love it. And she did.

The very last day arrived, and we were sad and a little happy also. Both of our teachers would be there. Looking back, I believe that Mrs. Scott needed a little moral support.

There was no work done that day. We could play board games or draw a picture or just visit quietly with our friends. It was really quiet for a fun day.

Mrs. Smith talked about how the class would be when we came back. We would keep the same rule and she liked it so well she would use it forever.

We would continue our studies as before and she would need our help. "You will have to be patient with me as I learn your names and how far you have progressed this year." Then she asked, "How many know their multiplication tables?" Only a few hands went up. She told us we would work on them.

She thanked Mrs. Scott for leaving her such a nice, well-behaved class. When the day was over, I think everyone was hugging and crying and then we went home. Christmas was of course wonderful. Filled with love and presents. Before gifts were opened dad read us about the birth of Jesus and why we celebrated Christmas. I loved to hear it read, it was not a story, it was the truth about the birth of our Savior.

We sang Silent Night and dad prayed. Then we opened presents. You have heard it said, a great time was had by all, and it was.

Vacation time was over, and it was time to go back to school. It was nice, it was fun, and we continued to learn.

Many times, a hand was raised, and someone would say that was not the way Mrs. Scott did it. I think Mrs. Smith got tired of hearing it. One day she said, "Let's try it my way for a while." Many times, we thought that it was not the way Mrs. Scott did it, but we did not say it again.

On the playground one day, I overheard a conversation between Mrs. Smith and another teacher. The other teacher was asking Mrs. Smith about her class. Her response was, "They are wonderful, but they will always be Mrs. Scott's class."

Mrs. Smith was a great teacher. There was a difference in our feelings for our third-grade teachers. We loved Mrs. Smith for being a good and nice teacher.

Our feelings for Mrs. Scott went much deeper.

We loved her not only as a great teacher but as a friend who loved us and was not afraid to show it.

Third grade, the middle of our journey through grade school was over and only time would tell what lay ahead.

Chapter 18

Another Summer

This was not just another summer.

It started out fantastic. Our families went camping together. We were gone for three weeks!

Each family rented a motorhome. It took a whole day for our moms to get them ready. They put clothes, they put blankets, they put games, they put pans, they put paper goods, and of course they put food and I don't know what else. I thought they would never get finished! Finally, the next morning, we were on our way.

Our first stop was Sequoia. If you have never been there, you have missed a wonderful experience. The forest was filled with GIANT REDWOOD TREES. I do mean giant! There was a tree so large that the center had been cut out and you could drive through it in a car. Our motorhomes were pretty large, so we did not try it, but we watched several cars drive through. I could hardly believe my eyes.

We stayed in the park for 4 days. We drove everywhere and we hiked and looked at everything. We saw deer and squirrels. Most of the time they stood still and watched us. I guess they were used to people. I waved goodbye as we drove away and hoped I could come back someday.

Next, we drove to Yosemite. Traveling was so much fun. We stopped several times at some beautiful spots to take pictures and just enjoy the view. Our moms took so many pictures, we had to stop several times to buy more film. That was ok because there was usually a café nearby where we could eat.

What can I tell you about the beauty of Yosemite? God's handiwork was everywhere. Trees, flowers, mushrooms, and animals. We stayed for a week and never saw it all. We hiked and rented bikes and rode everywhere. Well, not everywhere.

The next morning our moms cooked breakfast and we talked about where we should go next. There were so many places to see, and we only had a certain amount of time. Then Jimmy's dad said, "Have we thought about the Grand Canyon?" My dad thought it was a long way to Arizona. "We have a week left and it is only one day's drive," Jimmy's dad said. "Let's take a vote." To make a long story short we left after breakfast!

We stayed until it was time to come home. The last thing we did was awesome. We rode the Zip Lines.

I wish everyone could take this trip. Of course, everyone can't. I would like to share with you a poem my mom wrote. The title is Can't.

CAN'T

If you can't travel,
You can read a good book.

If you can't paint,
You can take a long look.

If you can't spell,
Your computer can check.

**If you don't have a pool,
You won't need a deck.**

**If you do have a smile,
You can give it away.**

**It could help someone else
To have a good day.**

  We came home happy and tired, but summer was not over. Our moms and dads were already planning for next summer. What great parents we have. We laughed and played and looked at the pictures our moms had taken. Then, all too soon, it was time for Fourth Grade.

Chapter 19

Frustration Steps In

I have never felt this way about school before! I was worried. If I struggled with math before, how would I be able to do better in fourth grade. Fourth grade was only three weeks away.

I talked about it to Jimmy, and he told me to talk to my parents. Good advice from my best friend.

As I spoke to them about my fears, mom cried. Then dad said, "Let's look on the internet and see if we can find a tutor for Timmy." How many kids have the blessings of parents like mine?

Dad stayed home from work, stayed on the internet and phone until he found a tutor skilled in math! I hope I will be a dad like that someday. The very next morning, Mrs. Dare came to our door. She came in and introduced herself. Everyone was smiling, even me.

She wasted no time; she gave me a few worksheets to complete. The tutor said they would help her understand where I needed help the most. After I finished, she looked them over carefully. After a few minutes she said, "Timmy, you can do simple addition and subtraction and you know your multiplication tables.

We will begin with multiplication and how to use it in problem solving." And we did. I will only say that I went into fourth grade with a smile, hoping for the best and knowing that I would try hard to learn more about math.

Chapter 20

Fourth Grade Begins

Jimmy and I were together again and ready for a new adventure.

We were really not concerned about the teacher. Other kids who had been in her class said she was very strict and very nice. Nice sounded fine but I was not so sure about strict. We soon found out!

Mrs. Barrie opened the door and said, "Clean your feet carefully on the mat before you come in, we must keep our room clean. It will be clean when you come in and clean when you leave for the day." WOW! She had not smiled yet. I had found the strict side but where was the nice? Our first day in fourth grade had begun.

She asked us to stand, and we would say the Pledge of Allegiance. Trouble! One boy who was new at our school said he did not want to say it.

"That is fine," said our teacher, "but, you will stand while the class says it, or you can explain to the principal why you do not want to follow the rules." He decided very quickly that standing would be the best thing to do. The new boy's name was David. He looked around as if to say, you better not laugh. No one did.

As the teacher called roll, she asked us to raise our hand when she called our name. Everyone did until she called David's name and he yelled, "Here!" Mrs. Barrie quickly responded, "I asked you to raise your hand! If I have to speak to you again you will get a referral and be sent to the principal's office." I will tell you this, that it never happened again.

Chapter 21

Kind Of Rules

"I believe we are going to have to post some rules on the board before we start our work," Mrs. Barrie said. "Who would like to help me?" Jimmy raised his hand and told the teacher that we only needed one rule.

For the first time she smiled. "How can that be," she said, "I really want to hear that one." "It is easy," said Jimmy, "we have to think." She had never heard that before. "I don't understand. What kind of a rule is that?"

Jimmy said, "I will show you," and he brought out a paper from his backpack. "I always keep a copy of this because it is very important." He showed her the paper. "That is wonderful," she said. "I will make a large chart of this and place it on the front board.

I especially like the K. We all need to be kind to each other."

"Would it be kind of me to let you go unpunished when you have done something wrong? NO, that would not be kind but wrong. We learn by our mistakes and try not to make them again. Will we be perfect and not do it again? No one is perfect but we can all be kind."

"I will try to be kind, but I will write your name on the board if you do something wrong and on purpose. If it is done again, you will get a check after it. The third time there will be a note home or a phone call to let your parents know about your behavior. If that does not work, you can have a little talk with the principal."

Let me say this, "I will be the kind of teacher you want. It will be your choice. I will be nice if you act like fourth grade students should, but I will always be strict about your behavior. Does that sound fair to you?" Everyone raised their hands including David.

Chapter 22

A Smile and A K!

The teacher smiled and the class smiled back. Kindness was here!

I even smiled when she said we were going to have math now. I could show kindness by trying hard.

Only the math books and the math workbooks were passed out. Then her question was this. How many of you know your multiplication tables? Several hands were raised. How many know them to five? More hands were raised.

Mrs. Barrie asked us to look at the first worksheet and said, "If anyone is not sure how to begin, please raise your hand. The first worksheet only uses multiplying to five. Please do your best and then tear them out carefully and place them on my desk. Take a few minutes to check out the next few pages while everyone finishes."

When everyone was finished the bell rang for recess.

Chapter 23

Learning Our Country

After recess it was time to get to work. Mrs. Barrie asked David and me to help pass out the books.

There were reading, science and social studies books. And of course, workbooks to go with them. We put them in our desks nicely which brought a smile from our teacher.

On one side of the room, she had placed a large map of the United States. It also included Canada and Mexico. There was also a map of Hawaii there.

She said she had been born in Mississippi and showed us on the map. She laughed and said you spelled it Miss iss ippi. We all spelled it with the teacher and laughed with her. Social Studies had begun. Then she gave us a tiny piece of paper to write our names on. The first one she called on was me. "Where were you born Timmy?" I said, "California." "Bring me your paper please," she said. I walked to the board, and she placed it right on California on the map.

Each child said where he or she was born, and she put it on the state. We had a variety of states with a name on them when she finished. What a great way to see our country.

We learned so many things about our country that year. We learned a little bit about the state and federal governments. Jamestown and the early years of our United States were part of our studies. I liked these lessons, especially about the Louisiana Purchase.

Using the large map on the wall we could see the states and the capital cities. Little did we know by our first look, we would have to learn the names of all the state capitals.

This was such a good time in my life, and I will not forget that nice and strict work well together.

Chapter 24

Reading and Writing

I had always been a good reader. However, I only read and had never paid much attention to what the parts of the sentences were and when to use commas and other marks.

I think we all knew nouns and verbs. What we were going to learn was pronouns, adverbs, and adjectives and where to use them and what they were for.

There were many pages in our workbooks to help us. They were to help us understand the characters by their actions and dialogue.

We wrote stories, rhymes, and book reports, to name a few. There were many tests to see if we were understanding about language and how to use it.

Only our best was acceptable work to our teacher! If there were too many mistakes in our writing, she would ask the student if it was their best. Usually, the answer was no. She corrected the papers, and they were done over to fix the mistakes. If the student was fooling around or not fixing the mistakes on the second paper, he or she would be setting outside the door at recess finishing with a clipboard. It did not take long for that to be a thing of the past.

Mrs. Barrie had a file for each student. On some days she would call a student up and show their files to them. She would show them a paper they had written the first of the year and one they had done last week. She would say how happy she was about their success and then she gave them a letter to their parents telling how proud she was of them.

What a thoughtful teacher! I wonder how many parents cried as they read this. How different from most letters home.

Chapter 25

Everything Else!

Let me back up just a little bit. A few words about math. It was VERY hard for me. Multiplying, dividing, fractions, decimals, and the hated word problems were a part of 4th grade. My math grades were never good, but my parents were very understanding and helped me as much as they could. They not only understood but went a step further. One evening every week the tutor came and helped me.

    Let's not go there again. Let's talk about the wonderful times in fourth grade! And there were many!

    We had art and we painted pictures. We used chalk and colored pencils also for our creations. We used glue and glitter and pens that wrote in gold or silver. We used stencils and our teacher brought us some wood cutouts at Christmas to paint and make into ornaments. She spent her own money to let us enjoy art and share it with our families.

We had music and P.E. We played many sports and did a lot of exercises. We went to the school library and checked out books.

We laughed and played and sang many patriotic songs.

Fourth grade was super…Our teacher was great…and our year was great! What else can I say. Now it was time to move on.

Chapter 26

Where Will We Go?

Three whole months of vacation. For Jimmy and me but not for our parents. They only had three weeks.

What we didn't know is that our parents had been planning this summer since our last trip!

Once again, our families rented motor homes. Everything we would need was already loaded when we came home from school on the last day of fourth grade!

We left early the next morning! Jimmy's folks let Jimmy ride with us until we stopped for breakfast. We asked where we were going and were told we would talk about it at breakfast.

We stopped at a small café where they pushed two tables together so we could eat and talk. Let me say this, "When you are traveling, don't pass up a small café for a better or nicer one. Just look where the large trucks are parked!!"

"Tell us where we are going," I said (a little too loud). Jimmy's dad laughed and said, "Quiet down and we will tell you."

"First, we are going to Arizona to see The Grand Canyon National Park. There is a lot to see so we will spend a few days there. We are going to Williams, Arizona for a special day. We are going on a train ride! It is called the Grand Canyon Railroad and we think it will be fun."

OH, FUN! We were traveling along (not singing a song) side by side enjoying the sights. Beautiful red rock formations were everywhere. The train traveled at a speed which let us enjoy the scenery. That is what it was for.

But then, a terrible thing happened! Can you believe this? The train was being robbed. Men with handkerchiefs over their faces were coming down the aisle and they had handguns. I was scared stiff until dad told me it was just an enactment of a train robbery, and the guns were not real. So, I just sat back and enjoyed it! What a ride!

Dinner and a night's rest and we were ready to see the park. We went to a visitor's center and hiked from there to Lipan Point where we could see the canyon and the Colorado River. There was white water rafting, but we only watched that. It looked a little scary to me but was fun to watch.

We stayed at the Grand Canyon for three days and were on the road again!

Where to now, we asked at breakfast. "I hope you don't mind riding for a while," said Jimmy's dad. "We are going to Wyoming!"

"What's in Wyoming?" I asked. "We are going fishing!" said dad. All the way to Wyoming I thought, we could fish a little way from home!

"Well, we are going to do a little more than just fish. WE ARE GOING TO YELLOWSTONE NATIONAL PARK!" dad said.

What can I tell you about this wonderful place? It is better than what you see on TV. My mom told us it covered nearly 3,500 square miles

We drove, hiked, and fished. We saw almost unbelievable sights. We visited canyons, alpine rivers, lush forests, hot springs, and geysers.

Old Faithful was our favorite geyser. It erupts every 44 minutes to 2 hours. We actually saw this happen.

On our travels throughout the park, we saw animals in the wild. We were told there were hundreds. We saw bears, one mama bear with her two cubs staring at us as we parked to watch. She was BIG.

We saw a pack of wolves, a few bison, elk, and antelope. We would always stop and watch them until they stopped watching us and left.

You could never see them all in one trip, probably not in many trips. Our last stop was the Museum of the Yellowstone which is in a train depot.

Our hearts filled to the brim with remembrances of our journey we began the trip home. One day we would travel this way again.

We spent the rest of the summer just doing what boys love to do. Playing, eating, and talking about our trip.

Then it was that time again. School was waiting. Fifth grade was waiting. How would that be? We could only wait and see.

Chapter 27

Wait And See

Jimmy and I walked to school together as we had been doing for several years. We talked as we walked. Jimmy was doing well but I was barely getting through math. He said he would help me all he could.

We did not know yet who our teacher would be, but we did know that we would be in the same class. We have been blessed to have wonderful teachers so far and we hoped for the best.

As we waited outside the door of our room, we wondered who would open it. We could only wait and see.

Chapter 28

A Fantastic Shock

Never in a million years would I have guessed who would open the door! The door opened quietly, and a person stepped out. IT WAS MRS. SCOTT!!!!

"What are you doing here we shouted?" With a smile she said, "Come in and you will find out!"

I don't know who was the happiest, Mrs. Scott or Jimmy or me, or many others. After we were seated, she told us her story.

She had gone back to school a few years before and got her teaching credential.

When she was our teacher, she was only a substitute teacher. Now, she had been hired full time and would teach at this school. SHE WOULD BE OUR TEACHER ALL YEAR!!!!

Chapter 29

Love And Joy!

Happy…Happy…Happy!

There were quite a few tears, mine and Jimmy's included to hear this news. We knew this year would be special.

Every person at this school seemed to be celebrating on this occasion. Everyone wore a smile. We knew we would have a fantastic year with a great teacher like Mrs. Scott.

The day started just like any school day. The Pledge of Allegiance and roll call. Next came the rules and out came the same board the teacher had made before. Time doesn't change everything!

Never has a first day been like this. Everyone smiling and willing to help. Mrs. Scott turned on some music and books and workbooks were passed out and put away.

Then something completely out of the ordinary came next. "I remember a student telling me about something when I was here before," the teacher said. "he said that he loved the Freeze Dance. I just happened to find this CD online, and I thought we would try it out! Everyone please line up around the outside of the desks and we will try it. Remember, you cannot move your feet and please be far enough from each other so you will not hit anyone with your hands."

Chapter 30

Please Not Now!

We had just begun our dance when the door opened. IT WAS THE PRINCIPAL!

"I thought I heard music coming from this classroom," Mrs. Gray said, "What is going on?" Before Mrs. Scott could speak, Jimmy raised his hand. Mrs. Gray nodded to him to speak.

Jimmy said, very nicely, "We are celebrating Mrs. Scott's returning to this school and being our teacher."

It will be hard for you to believe what happened next. The principal told us the whole school was happy to have her back and she smiled. "Would you mind if I joined you?" she said. So, the kids danced, the teacher danced, and the principal danced. What a morning!

We laughed and then went to our desks and our work began.

"Please open your reading books and read the first story. Then complete the worksheets which are about the story. I am going to set down and rest now while you work," she said with a smile.

You remember David, don't you? He had not had Mrs. Scott for a teacher so I guess he was going to try her out. He spoke very loudly and said he needed to go to the bathroom. No raising of his hand, just a loud voice.

Mrs. Scott looked at him for at least a minute and then she spoke. "Excuse me," she said, "Do you know how to read?" He said that he did, and she told him to read the rules posted on the front board to the class.

David looked very funny and said, "Now?"

She told him, "Yes and please stand up." After he read them out loud, she asked him if he knew how to follow rules.

Admitting he did, David, (still standing) was turning a little red and speaking very nicely. "Please follow them or face the consequences," was what she told him. "Sit down please and we will complete our lesson."

We finished our work, and it was time for recess.

Chapter 31

Recess Talk and Play

As we left the room, I asked David if Jimmy and I could talk to him. I said we would like to be his friends.

"Why?" he said, "I have not been very nice today. I am sorry for acting up in class. Mrs. Scott seems to be very nice."

Then we filled him in! "Mrs. Scott is the nicest, the best, the fairest, and the most loving of any teacher you will ever have." We told him about our time with her and how happy we had been.

Then we said, "Let's play!" And we did and soon became friends. What a difference a play makes!

Chapter 32

Kindness

We three boys entered the room after recess to see our lesson written on the board, PLEASE TAKE OUT YOUR MATH BOOKS QUIETLY.

Then our teacher asked us how many liked math. Unbelievable, a few hands were raised. The next question was how many of you hate math. A lot more hands came up. "Would you like it better if you knew how to do it?" Almost every hand went up.

"I am going to try to help you like math a little better," she said.

"We have 20 students in this room so I am going to put you into 5 groups of 4 so you can help each other. I need 5 of you who like and are good at math to please raise your hands." Jimmy was one of the five.

One of these would be in each group and everyone in the group would help each other. Some were better in some parts of math than the other ones. "This is to be a work group not a fun group and we will try it for two weeks and see if it works," Mrs. Scott said.

Today, we will work at our desks and finish the first two pages in the math workbook. When you have finished, please tear them out and place them in the math basket as you leave for lunch. If you finish before the bell rings you may quietly select a book from our class library bookshelf and read." Work completed we went to lunch.

Chapter 33

Happiness Shared

Jimmy, and I and our new friend David had played hard after lunch and were pretty hot and tired.

It was a hot day outside and Mrs. Scott had turned the air conditioning on. It felt very good. She told us to sit quietly, and she would tell us a little about herself. "Many of you already know me and I hope are happy to have me as your teacher again, I always wanted to be a teacher and I was 55 when I decided to return to school and make my dream come true. I worked hard and it took me 5 years to complete my work."

Mrs. Scott said, "It is never too late to make a dream come true. But I do not want you to wait for yours to happen. Now is the beginning of YOUR time. What you learn now will help you reach your goal."

"But this is only fifth grade, how will this help us?" asked Beverly. Our teacher smiled and told her to think about first grade. "Did you know everything then that you know now?" she asked. Her answer was, "of course not." Mrs. Scott said, "Pretend you are on a ladder, and you can only take one step at a time. With each step you take you are closer to your dream. You learn every step of the way and your knowledge continues to grow.

Reaching my goal has filled my life with love and happiness."

"Tell me something that has made you happy," said Mrs. Scott.

The first hand that was raised was David's.

This is what he said, "I have never started a school year being happy. I thought I had to do something to make me feel important and impress the class. What I have found today is TWO NEW FRIENDS. I have also found a teacher who cares about her class. I am so happy I can hardly hold it. Thank you, Timmy, and Jimmy."

"Thank you, David, for sharing that with us." Mrs. Scott said. "I loved it."

Chapter 34

School Continues

"Now, we need to get to work to take another step up. Please take out your reading book and read the first story. It is a historical story about the Liberty Bell. Then continue with your workbook and complete the two pages about the story."

Mrs. Scott continued, "You are going to find that you will be doing more individual work in those books than before. Just remember that I am always here if you need help."

Our whole class worked quietly for the next hour and then it was time for lunch, and boy was I hungry. We were having lunch a little later than the lower grades. When I was finished eating, I was so full I did not want to run the track or play tether ball, so some friends and I just walked and talked. The bell rang and we went to work on this step up the ladder.

Chapter 35

Discussion Time

"Let's take a little time and talk about what you already know and what you will learn this year," Mrs. Scott said. Then she asked, "who would like to tell me what you know about math?" I sat on my hands and hoped she would not call on me.

Jimmy raised his hand and told her that we had learned more about fractions and decimals. We had also learned about triangles. "Many," he said, "knew that the word problems had gotten very hard, and some were having trouble with them." The teacher said, "Thank you Jimmy, I will try to think of a way to help the class with them."

"Let's talk about science now. How were your science studies?" One girl said we talked about plant life cycles, and she loved that. She told us how she had gone home, and she and her mother and sister had planted flower seeds in a window box and watched them grow. "I watched them every day as they came up as little shoots and grew until we had beautiful flowers," she said.

"I love planting and watching flowers and vegetables grow from tiny seeds," Mrs. Scott told us.

"Let's talk about Social Studies next. Tell me about that." My hand was one of the first ones up. "Tell us what you liked about social studies Timmy," she said.

"I loved reading about Jamestown and the early years," I said, "but being able to identify the fifty states was hard." Social Studies was one of my best subjects I told the class.

"I love reading and learning about the states too," she said. "How many like Social Studies?" Almost every hand was raised. "You are going to love it this year," she said. "We are going to read and learn more about the beginning of our country."

"Oh," she said, "There is so much to talk about! The 13 colonies…the American Revolution…The Boston Tea Party and so much more. This is a subject you will love!"

"MY goodness," she exclaimed! "It is time for my class to have P.E. Follow me."

P.E. was fun. The teacher began with exercises and then a run around the track.

I, for one, was a little tired but I stuck with it. Then we just shot a few baskets or played tether ball until the bell rang. Back to class and making sure everything was put away and the day was over.

Several friends walked home together and talked about our first day. We were all happy to be in Mrs. Scott's room and believed that this year would be good. Then Jimmy said, "Yep, we have to climb that ladder." and everyone laughed.

There were so many good times, so much happiness and so much love in our class that year. We learned so many things about our country, and about each other.

It wasn't all about math and reading and social studies and science. We learned how to work together in groups. It was about strengthening friendships and families and neighbors. I look back of fifth grade as one of the high spots of my life!

Chapter 36

Another Summer

What would we do this summer Jimmy and I wondered? What else was there to do? Our parents were busy talking to each other and told us to go to Jimmy's house and find something to do as they were busy. We wanted to hear what they were talking about. No such luck! "Go and play at our house," said Jimmy's mom, "and there are some chocolate chip cookies in the kitchen that I made for you this morning."

This was not a good way to spend the first day of our summer we said to each other. We had been left out! We were old enough to take care of ourselves at home! We did have pizza that evening together and that was nice. But every once in a while, one of the moms would giggle.

Chapter 37

Wow!

Jimmy stayed at my house that night and we put a puzzle together on the kitchen table while our parents were outside talking and laughing AGAIN. What was up?

We woke up to the smell of bacon frying and grownups talking. We dressed and went down for breakfast. Everyone was smiling and then dad said, "Have you looked out the window this morning?"

We ran to look out and there they were. Two large motorhomes. We both screamed at the same time, "Where are we going?"

"Sit down and eat breakfast and we will talk about it. Then we'll have to get busy and get ready for our trip!"

Jimmy's dad said, "You boys have been talking about what you have been learning about our country in school this year and we have planned something we think you will love. We are going to take a road trip and see more of our country. Does that sound good?"

Chapter 38

Unimaginable Fun

It didn't take long for us to pack the motorhomes as our parents had been getting ready for weeks. Within two hours we were on the road. Jimmy rode with us until we stopped and ate the lunch our moms had made for us and then I rode with him. We spent most of the time looking out the windows and talking. No one had told us where we were going. We were just happy to be going together. I did think about Laddie and hoped he was ok at a friend's house. Then, I guess the excitement took its toll. We both took a nap.

The next morning, we drove until we found a small café where a lot of trucks were parked and stopped there. While we were eating, our parents asked if we would like to see the capital of our nation. We squealed like babies. "YES," we said, "How long will it take?"

It took several days, and we spent time sightseeing along the way. We wanted to

see every new place we hadn't seen before.
Late one afternoon we were there!!

Chapter 39

The Sights We Saw

The first thing we did was park in a nice motorhome park and rent a large car so we could see the sights together. And did we see them! Our parents had a notebook they had put together to help us see everything. Well, not everything! As I thought about it later, I knew it would take many trips to see only part of it.

"Let's go to the National Mall Memorial while it is still daylight," said my mom.

I was glad we had a car which guided us to the different places, or we would never have found our way around. After we parked, we found the elevator and went up 500 feet for the best view of the city. AWESOME! "We will never be able to see all of this," my dad told us. "We will talk together about what we really want to see tonight. We have picked up some folders about the sights and we will look at them and decide."

After dinner we started looking at them. I spotted one first that I wanted to visit. "Look at all these planes," I told Jimmy. We were so excited that my parents said we would go there tomorrow. It was called the Air and Space Museum and it was fantastic.

Our moms had a choice also and they wanted to go to the National Arboretum which had multiple gardens and we could take a picnic lunch. Dad said, "you can see flowers anywhere." One look at mom's face and he quickly changed his mind. "Oh, look," he told us, "This pamphlet says sometimes you can see a bald eagle there. Let's go in the morning and then go to the museum." Smart dad!

We spent many days in the capital and saw so many things I can't even remember all of them.

We went to the Washington Monument, the Capital Building, Library of Congress, Supreme Court Building, and the Lincoln and Thomas Jefferson Memorials.

We went to the Smithsonian National Museum and then we went to what our dad's called a special place, Arlington National Cemetery.

I had been to a cemetery before but not one like this. It covered miles and miles. We all shed a few tears when our parents told us about the many wars that these men had served in so we could be free. We must never forget the men who served to keep America free.

We saw the changing of the guards at the Tomb of the Unknown Soldier. My dad found out about the changing of the guards on his computer. I was so glad we were there to see it.

(The Changing of the Guard. The military guard at the Tomb of the Unknown Soldier is changed in an elaborate ceremony which happens every hour on the hour from October 1 through March 31, and every half hour from April 1 through September 30).

We left Washington D.C. and saw many great places on our trip. We were on our way again. We were going to see where our country began. We only had time to visit 7 of the original 13 colonies. We also saw the Liberty Bell.

Just two weeks and four days after we left home, we parked in front of our houses. We were almost too tired to get out. Everyone slept late the next morning and after breakfast we unloaded the motorhomes. Our dad's vacations were over, but we had the rest of the summer to enjoy. WE DID.

We met friends at the park close to home and played baseball. No, not just kids, there was always a parent watching and sometimes joining in. They were not that good. Don't tell them I said that!

There were always Saturdays to spend together with our families. Friday evenings we traveled closer to home. We stayed at a motel and had Saturday to enjoy a new or well-known place.

Many overnight trips were spent at the beach. I remember the day we saw what looked like hundreds of sea gulls flying and landing on the beach. What a sight to behold. One Friday we went to Catalina Island. It was wonderful!

I will tell you one thing. We always went to church on Sunday!

Chapter 40

A New Day

It seemed to come too quickly. We were getting SO grown up. I think both Jimmy and I grew an inch over summer.

How will sixth grade be we wondered. Would this next step up the ladder be harder than the others? Who would our teacher be? We had signed up to be in the same room again and we would be sad if one of us was changed.

We went to the room we had asked for and there it was. A class list posted on the door. HURRAY! We were both there. Everyone in line was smiling…until the door opened.

As it opened, we stared at a six-foot-tall young man with blond hair and blue eyes! He smiled and said, "Come on in. I am your new teacher. My name is George…I mean Mr. Jones."

We were surprised, to say the least, as we had only had women teachers before. In fact, there was only one other male teacher in the school, and we had heard he was very strict. What were we in for?

He told us to take a seat where we wanted, and he would see how that worked out. If we were quiet and well behaved, we could stay there. If not, we would be moved. It was our choice!

Mr. Jones took roll first and then we said the Pledge of Allegiance. As the class sat down, our teacher remained standing and said this, "I like students to work in groups as much as possible but that will take a while to get to know one another. This is my first year at this school and it will be your last. Let's make it a good one."

"Just as there are rules in life, there will be rules in this classroom. Does anyone have a rule we could use?" he continued. This was Jimmy's time to raise his hand. Mr. Jones nodded, and Jimmy took his rule sheet out of his backpack and handed it to him. As he read it, he said, "Hmm. This looks pretty good. Does anyone else have something?" This was my time, and I was ready. I had pulled my sheet out and I handed it to him. "Hmm. This looks good also. I will look these over and we will talk about rules later."

"I need three young men to pass out the books that are lined up on the back cabinet. They are heavy, so be careful and take a few at a time. Pass the reading books first and the reading workbooks. When you are finished with these please sit down and we will get to the others later."

"As soon as you receive your book, please read the first story. You will find it is much longer than in other grades and you need to read it carefully as you will be having a quick test on it before recess. I will allow you 35 minutes to read it and then we will have the test." A few students looked at each other in alarm. We had never done this before.

Thirty-five minutes later Mr. Jones said, "Please put your books way and take out your pencil and I will pass out the tests. Any tests that come back without a name will automatically receive an F."

It was a multiple-choice test which helped. It was not that hard if you had read and understood the story. The teacher said,

"Please sit quietly when you are finished so you will not disturb the others. We only have a few minutes until recess. When the bell rings, I will dismiss you a row at a time. Those not finished please stay and continue." Everyone finished.

Chapter 41

Help Please

We were very quiet at recess. Our whole class, even the girls, talked about sixth grade. What will it be like to have a man teacher? Will we even like him? Will he be fun and maybe just a little funny, or STRICT? We decided we would do our best because we were almost grown up. We thought!

Returning to class we were told that after we have talked a little, he would send a seating chart around for each one to put their names on. He would need this to be able to learn and remember them.

"I am going to ask you for help, please listen. This is only my second year of teaching and my first teaching sixth grade. I will do everything I can to help you succeed this year and you can help me also. We can learn sixth grade together. Is everyone ok with that?" Everyone smiled and said "yes," and a happy day started. We would all work together.

He told us this. "I looked at the rules the two boys showed me and wrote them both on the board. I really liked both and could not decide which to use."

"Shall we vote on them? Raise your hand if you like number one." Every hand was raised. "Well, it looks like number one has won." Then Billy raised his hand and said we should also vote on number two. "It has already been decided," the teacher said. "Can we just vote anyway," Billy asked? "OK," the teacher said. "Who likes number two?" Again, every hand was raised. Mr. Jones had a puzzled look on his face. Billy raised his hand again and said, "Can we please use them both so we will never forget them?"

An unforgettable smile crossed Mr. Jones face and his eyes sparkled. "What a help this class has been already. Of course, we can, and I will make each of you a copy to take home."

"Are we ready for math? Would you boys that I point to pass out he books needed for math and we will begin." When this was finished, I raised my hand and told him I had a hard time with math. He asked if anyone else was struggling with math and several hands were raised.

The teacher seemed a little puzzled and said, "Let me think about this and we will talk more tomorrow. But now look at the first two pages in your math workbook and complete them. This will help me understand where you need the most help. When you are finished, tear them out and bring them to me."

Before we began, he asked us to get a book from the bookcase on the side of the room and take it to our desk. "You will do this one row at a time. Don't be choosy, you can change it later. Just in case you finish your math early you will have something to do." The mornings work was finished, and we knew that we would like grade six. Then the bell rang for lunch.

After lunch a bunch of hot kids hit the room. "Sit down and cool off," Mr. Jones told us. "We have all worked hard this morning, so I say let's take some time off. Some of you can tell what you did last summer during vacation time."

We spent the remainder of the day just getting to know each other. Great day! Every child had something to say. All had been ready to come back to school as they had missed their friends and were looking forward to sixth grade. Everyone was excited to talk about their summer fun. Different families, different places, each kid had their own story.

We finished the first day with a half sheet of construction paper and markers to draw a picture of where we had been. This had been a sort of lazy day but tomorrow would be another day.

Chapter 42

Struggle and Learn

Mr. Jones was nice, he was caring, he was forgiving, to a point. I will tell you about this later. One thing he did do was he kept our noses to the grindstone (I heard this saying from my dad). It means he kept us busy and because he did his best to teach us, he expected us to do our best to follow instructions and learn.

We had a lot to learn! We had science, math, P.E., language arts, social studies, music, art and more. There were times when it almost seemed too much. Mr. Jones was a great teacher and led us slowly through each of our subjects. We never had all of them on the same day which was good.

Math and language arts were hard, but we were going a step further up from what we already knew.

Social studies were a bit different. Last year we learned about our country. This year we were learning a little about the world! Science was fun and we were able to understand a little more as time went on.

Let's get back to math for a minute. Mr. Jones said he would stay for one hour after school on Mondays to help those struggling with math. We would need a signed note from our parents that we could stay. They could also come and help if they wanted. What a guy! There were 4 boys and 3 girls that needed help. This was every Monday of every week of our sixth grade! He taught, we listened, and we began to understand.

Math will never be my favorite subject, understanding how it worked was a blessing I will remember. Mr. Jones was a success as a friend and teacher.

Before I leave sixth grade, I must tell you how he settled one problem. We had both sets of rules on the board. However, over time a few got a little neglectful and had to have the process of their names on the board, then a check and a few times a call home.

I remember it was on a Monday. As we came into the room, every child's name was on the side chalkboard. "Why?" we asked, "we have been good!" "We will talk about it later," said our teacher. We waited and nothing was said. Then a boy got his name on the board. That was nothing new, it had been there before. A little later he had a check beside it. The next time he got out of line Mr. Jones stood up, went to the side chalkboard, and erased his name! Very softly he said, "it will take three days of good behavior to get your name back up with the great students!" I believe the boy made it! This board was a place of honor. Encouragement is always helpful.

Chapter 43

Awards, Tears and A Step Up

There was a great celebration for the sixth-grade graduation. All the parents were invited, and lunch was served to everyone.

There were awards for about anything you could think of. Every student took a certificate home that day. No one was left out. I got the best readers award and Jimmy the math award. I heard our parents say as we left the school for the last time. I TOLD YOU THEY WERE SUPER SMART. ONE MORE STEP UP THE LADDER!

Chapter 44

A Long Look Back

Timmy has grown a lot. He has spent a total of seven years at the same school. From kindergarten we have seen him grow, make friends, and have many happy times.

In this fictional series, this is a great help for a great future. In real life it is also a blessing. Let's take a look at other children to see the difference in lifestyles.

Just as Jimmy moved to a new town so many children live a life that is constantly moving. It can be very hard to make new friends and get settled in a new place.

I believe, that as parents we should help children to show kindness to new students. That doesn't mean they should make them good friends immediately. Just remember that the K stands for kind.

Chapter 45

Another Summer!

Our families spent many happy times together that summer. We traveled in motor homes again and saw many places in California and Arizona.

Our parents had talked about where we would spend this vacation. They decided we would not travel so far this year. They had found many exciting places that were closer to home.

They decided to go to Death Valley National Park first before it became too hot to enjoy. They had made reservations at a private R.V. park where we would spend three nights. The name was Stovepipe Wells. Once again, they had rented a large car so we could spend our time together.

I asked why it would be so hot there. Dad told me that it was the lowest, driest, and hottest area in North America and was below sea level. IT WAS HOT! But our car was cool, and we made many stops. We did not stay out in the sun very long on these stops. Even though it was so hot, you could see for miles around and see snow caps on the far distant mountains.

    Back in the motorhomes we traveled to San Francisco. And the sights we saw! We drove across the Golden Gate Bridge. We went to China Town, and we rode the trolly cars. We went to the waterfront and then went on a bay cruise. We even went to Alcatraz Island. I really did not like that very much.

    We saw so many places that summer. Santa Catalina Island again, Lake Tahoe, the Monterey Aquarium which we all liked, and The San Diego Zoo. Jimmy's dad said, "We have saved something special to do before we go home. We are going on the Verde Canyon Railroad Adventure!"

    We traveled home with awe for the sights we had seen together. Our hearts were filled with love and happiness. It would soon be time for a large change in our lives. Going from elementary school to Jr. High was a little scary!

Epilogue

The years of 2020 and 2021 have been difficult years for many. Covid, face masks, school on the internet, inflation and so many trials to overcome. But through it all we are still AMERICA. We are blessed to live in this country. I am very happy and thankful for four of the most wonderful grown children that a mother could be blessed with. One of my children is a fifth-grade teacher who loves teaching as much as I do. She has written a poem for her students as they leave fifth grade and continue their education. I would love to share it with you.

Mrs. Prasser's Poem

A worldwide pandemic is how we started the year
Face masks and shields were part of our gear
When you entered this class, you were filled with unrest

But within a few days you were doing
your best
We had much work to do to get you
engaged
A year at home on the computer
caused your brain to age
Language arts came first with phonics
and reading
Oh, my what a task, Mrs. Prasser
always pleading
Remember your vowels! Read at home
in the den
If you can't read our books your future
is grim
The writing was hard and didn't make
sense
When I said, "go rewrite it" you
wanted to go jump the fence
But you all persevered and continued
to try
The writing was much better now no
need to cry
Then came the math struggle number
two
I begged and I pleaded,
"multiplication you must do!"

Some heeded my warning and put in the time
Others dug in and refused so confused it was a crime
But finally in May, most were tired of not knowing
They finally learned their times tables and the progress was showing
We celebrated the holidays and tried to get in the mood
But the office explained "You must party without food"
As I send you ahead to sixth grade all prepared
Remember what you've learned and please don't be scared
I've taught you to believe and never give up trying
Keep your future in sight and never stop flying

Love, Mrs. Prasser

My Thank You

My sincere thanks to Hazel and Scott for their encouragement and the support they have given me. They not only encouraged me but told me I had to write more!

My family has been with me all the way with their love and encouragement. I may get a phone call from one of my children asking, how is Timmy today? Isn't that cute! I tell them how far in school he is, and we laugh together. Hannah, you are so sweet and a great artist. Thank you for the wonderful book covers which tell a story before the book is even opened!

My most important thank you is to my Lord Jesus who died for me and has blessed me with 88 years on earth. Thank you, Lord.

Made in United States
Orlando, FL
17 June 2023